D1431085

Fighting to Live: How to thrive Inside & Outside of Ministry

The Handbook for Pastors' Wives, Women in Ministry
& Leadership

By Pastor Valerie T. Frazier

ISBN: 978-0-9982141-0-8

Published by
Free Mind Publishing-A Self-Publishing Service
P.O. Box 973
Wake Forest, NC 27588
www.freemindpublishing.com

Table of Contents

Acknowledgements

To my loving husband, Pastor Rodney E. Frazier, Sr., thank you for being my rock and anchor in the earth. You are truly a man of integrity and humility.

To my firstborn, Rodney E. Frazier II, you are my pride. I will always adore your charm, humor, and wit. You have such a special place in my heart.

To my joy, Christina Frazier Mason, go forth and lead your generation to a place of worship that is in spirit and truth. Many blessings to you & Cadarreus.

To my sisters, Cheryl, Bonnie, Christie and Katriel, so thankful to be born into a community of real sisterly love and support. To my brother Milton, all my nieces and nephews, always keep God first!

To Kingdom Family International Church, I am eternally grateful for every "do over" I was given! And to every Pastor, Pastor's wife, Minister, and Minister's wife, stay focus on *your* assignment. Your uniqueness is a gift to the world.

Dedication

This book is dedicated to my parents Milton & Cherry Tripp who recently celebrated 57 Years of marriage. You are my inspiration. I love you both.

Other books by Pastor Valerie T. Frazier

Falling Forward: Raising Selfless Children in a Self-Centered Society.

Marriage on Purpose: How to Ignite Your Marriage & Keep the Fire Burning

Audio Teachings by Pastor Valerie T. Frazier

Great Comeback of the Church-Part I & II

The Power of Imagination

Celebrating African American History

Divine Birth Experience

Identity Crisis

Pastor Valerie Frazier, CCLC
Women's Pastor, Kingdom Family International Church
Certified Christian Life Coach
For more information on Pastor Valerie T. Frazier and her upcoming events visit:
www.valeriefrazier.org
www.kingdomfamily.church

Preface

Ephesians 4:11 states, "He Himself gave some to be apostles, some prophets, some evangelists, and some Pastors and teachers," This can also be read, He gifted the Body of Christ with leaders in the form of apostles, some prophets, some evangelists, and some pastors and teachers. What an honored to be called a gift from God.

What joy these assignments privilege us as we stand before precious men and women of God. Teaching humankind the principles and laws of God results in them leading spiritually profitable and productive lives. This aids them in fulfilling their personal assignments and purposes.

Additionally, as gifts to the body we are occasionally showered during special occasions and reminded of the lives that we impact and change. Humility is the key as this calling comes with bumps, bruises, disappointments, missteps and yes, some regrets. It is during these times that I am reminded of words my husband often states: "You are not as good as they say you are and not as bad as you think you are." Nevertheless, keep the faith with the goal in mind of hearing "well done thy good and faithful servant" from the one whom we serve and glorify.

I have been led to write this handbook to assist Pastors' wives, Ministers' wives, female Pastors and Ministers. If you fit in any of these categories, I encourage you to take the time and read this book for your personal edification. If you or someone you know is considering the call to ministry or are yoked to someone answering the call, this book will be a great help. Oh how I wish I had a handbook as I blindly walked into my place of destiny.

Some time ago, I was invited to be the keynote speaker at an International Women's Conference in Siaya, Kenya, Africa. One session was designated for me to speak to the female Pastors and Pastor's wives at Future Life Christian Ministries. In preparation for this assignment, I explored the internet and visited several local bookstores in search of a handbook covering this subject matter. The one book that was available was so outdated that I should have never purchased it. In desperation, after having purchase the book, I proceeded to read that work without obtaining much pertinent information for the time we live in. It is my prayer that you read and enjoy the information in this work as much as I enjoyed sharing my knowledge and personal experiences with each of you. By no means does this publication insinuate that I am an authority in pastoring a church. However, my short 12 years has been a learning curve I felt led to share with those who are interested. I have selected topics on everything I wished I had advance knowledge of while supporting my husband and fulfilling my personal call of ministry. I appreciate it all now more than ever as we pursue our Kingdom Purposes.

Chapter 1: Valley of Decisions

"...For the day of the Lord is near in the valley of decision."

Joel 3:14

The book of Joel speaks of a valley called *decisions*. On this day, the Lord will make a decision concerning those who have obeyed and are with Him and those who are against Him. It is critical to know you have to work out your own soul salvation and you must do this with fear and trembling.

> *"Therefore, my beloved, as you have always obeyed, not as in my presence only, but now much more in my absence, work out your own salvation with fear and trembling." (Philippians 2:12 NKJV)*

Regardless of what your spouse, co-laborers, or congregation does or how they treat you, you will ultimately stand before a righteous God to give an account of your life. There is no option to stand alongside your life partner, explaining what you did or did not do because of their actions. It is required that you be cautiously prayerful about the significant other with whom you agree to be equally yoked.

Your significant other will share in your public triumphs and defeats. Who do you really want on the front line with you? This person has a front row seat to your insecurities and shortcomings. Can the person you are selecting be trusted with this sensitive information? Will they have the capacity and ability to love your insecurities out of you and build you up? In the same respect, are you willingly yoking yourself to an individual who perhaps have studied these character flaws to take advantage of them for their own selfish and perverted motives?

ARE YOU READY FOR SOME REAL TALK? IF SO, PROCEED WITH CAUTION.

Considering all things, there are times when people do not think through to the other side of choosing a spouse. Consuming thoughts of flowery wedding day details and the goal of fleeing the trappings of the sexual sin of fornication becomes the focus, resulting in hasty decisions.

As you stand in the valley of decision concerning who you will take on as your spouse, there is much to consider. Are you confident that the two of you will commit to one another from that day forward? Take to heart the following words "for better, for WORSE, for richer, for POORER, in SICKNESS and in health, until death do you part". Are you truly ready to commit to them all? Marriage is a huge leap of faith and you must consider all it entails. Hebrews 11:1 tells us *"Now faith is the substance of things hoped for, the evidence of things not seen."*[1]

The New Living Translation of the Bible states it like this *"Faith is the confidence that what we hope for will actually happen; it gives us assurance about things we cannot see."*

Consequently, have you evaluated the substance in your potential mate? What is the substance that makes them who they are? Have you assessed your evidence or clearly quantified their reputation? It is important to evaluate your potential mate while you are dating and assess whether they can go where God is calling you to go. Are you willingly preparing to stand with them as they go where God is taking them? Joining to a mate and dragging them to one's place of destiny can become an unwanted lifelong challenge.

---

[1] Hebrews 11:1 King James Version

5

"The race is not given to the swift nor the battle to the strong, neither yet bread to the wise, nor yet riches to men of understanding, nor yet favour to men of skill; but time and chance happeneth to them all." (Ecclesiastes 9:11 KJV)

The joy in living is making sure your timing is God's timing and your chance is laced in faith in Him. The truth is there is an adversary who is working against you. Your spouse should be committed to joining you in fighting against the enemy. We should walk in a level of discernment that will alert us to when the enemy is trying to use us as a pawn against one another. Negligent recognition of the attempts of the enemy to use a spouse against another happens often. Personal example, my husband and I were Marriage Couple Leaders at our former church, 'Fulfilled Promise Tabernacle'. It went without fail that the week we were to teach a session, we would find ourselves engaging in explosive disagreements. It was like clockwork until we recognized this pattern of the enemy and took authority over his plan of destruction.

We would be on the alert and ahead of this tactic and disband him accordingly.

In retrospect, a godly spouse is one who accepts the core person you are while encouraging you to be the best you are to be...in Christ. Notice I said *in Christ* and not "in the world".

One of the vices the enemy uses to position spouses against one another is TV, Reality TV to be specific. Reality TV has ushered in a cloud of confusion not only in the world but also in the church...yes the church. Reality TV promotes false and unrealistic expectations in the marriage union on you and your spouse. In some instances, we are tempted with trying to live out all the seasons of life at once, as they are glamourized and mimicked on television. In many cases, people want their spouses to reflect the ones they see on television and the televangelist broadcasts. Having no clue of who the person actually is in reality. People fall in admiration with the TV "personality" they think they know through media outlets and taint their reality with this viewed fantasy.

The unsolicited advice to you is to be who you are and allow your spouse to do the same. No one desires to be married to an individual who constantly opposes who they are or who they are supposed to be in Christ. Only the person who accepts you at your worst deserves you at your best. Everyone is a work in progress and deserve a bit of grace as they "yet become" in Him.

If you are engaged to be married to an individual that wants to inflict their self-imposed makeover on you, you may want to go back to God for some wisdom and guidance. Here are some important things to do:

1. Spend time fasting and praying concerning your decision.

2. Consult a trusted friend who has a proven track record in walking in truth, making godly decisions and giving out godly advice.

3. Seek additional godly counsel to discuss your concerns and any red flags that have presented themselves.

4. Pre-Engagement counsel will prove to be profitable as well. This should take place well before rings are purchased and dates are set.

Once you have done this, make a decision you are prepared to live with. It is not impossible to accomplish your God given assignment with a spouse who is more of a burden than a blessing. However, it will come with much heartache, self-imposed challenges, tears, and less of the abundant life promised to you.

If you think, you are called to be a Pastor and you are dating or engaged to a Pastor, there are some decisions that need to be made before you embark upon this new adventure. If you do not, **"Prepare"** in advance to walk down this path, you are laying the groundwork for seasons of struggle. People marry promising each other the sun, moon, and stars. These promises may quickly diminish their brightness without effective pre-marriage counseling.

One of the greatest gifts my husband and I gave each other was premarital counseling. In an honest assessment, without the wisdom shared by our then Pastor Dr. Shelton Murphy, we probably would not be joyfully married and enjoying a time of reinventing ourselves in this season of *emptying the nest*. Our premarital counseling sessions provoked us into taking multiple self-assessments and forced us to respond to very challenging questions beforehand. Spiritual insight proves to be more profitable than hindsight in some cases.

Walking along the path of spiritual insight will force you to walk in each other's truth. You have to examine each of your family trees to see what fugitives are harboring in your generational bloodlines. Taking the time to reflect and examine your family tree or patterns of behavior, you can see which are repetitive. These behaviors permit blessings and sometimes curses. A godly heritage is handed from generation to generation. God allows both blessings as well as curses.

> *"...I, the LORD your God, am a jealous God, visiting the iniquity of the fathers upon the children unto the third and the fourth generations of them that hate*

me, and shewing mercy unto thousands
of them that love me and keep my
commandments." (Deuteronomy 5:9-
10)[2]

Be clearly aware of the level of warfare you may be exposed to. Prepare yourself to join forces, come against, and defeat the enemy, who is no stranger to attacking the institution of marriage.

Getting to know your mate's family generationally should be followed up by attendance in continuing married couples' ministry classes provided by your local church[3]. It is amazing how married couples struggle inside and outside of the church, while most churches do not provide or put emphasis on marriage ministry.

Many people enroll themselves in self-help classes and continuing education classes for a job, but fail to "tune-up" their marriages. Cosmetologist and many other professions require you to renew your licenses after a period of time. Tune-ups in marriages are

---

[2] [of generations, see 7:9]
[3] All of the suggestions are based on personal experience yielding results of a lasting marriage.

needed if you want your marriage to thrive and not just survive. It is important to spend some time fasting, praying, and seeking God to reveal the life plan He has laid out for you existing before he created the foundations of the earth. He is a Rewarder of those who diligently seek Him (Hebrew 11:6). This is true as an individual as well as in your marriage. Once this is revealed share your discovery with each other. In your discovery reflect on these questions; is there a call to Pastor or become a Minister? Is your fiancé/fiancée comfortable with you entering into the ministry? Is he/she comfortable watching you be exalted as he/she is called to support or be a Lay Minister? Are you comfortable ministering together while avoiding the spirit of competition? Can the two of you see one another be all God has called you to be and continue to live in peace? Do you like each other enough? These are the sorts of questions that you should formulate honest responses to before saying "I do".

Marriage and Ministry are complicated and extremely challenging. Marriage does not effectively work with two broken people trying to come together to become one whole. It is two whole people coming together as one. In other words, the true joys of marriage & ministry produce phenomenal results when both husband and wife know the word, apply the word, and allow it to transform them. This is how they are able to walk in agreement. Can two walk together and not agree? (Amos 3:3 *paraphrased*)

Marriage is definitely not for the faint of heart. Our prayers before God concerning marriage should be similar to the following prayers.

Praying the word...

Men: Father God, lead me to the woman suitable for me. As I submit to you, lead me to the woman that will submit to me and fit into the plan of God for my life. Teach me how to love her as you loved the church. Teach me how to love myself, so I can love her as my own body. Thank you for allowing us to become one flesh.

Women: Father God, let me be found by the man that I am suitable for. As he submits to you, teach me how to submit to him while fitting into his plan and completing the call of God on my life. Thank you for showing me how to respect my husband and allowing me to become one flesh with him.

In Jesus name, Amen.[4]

[4] Genesis 2:18, Ephesian 5:22-33

Chapter 2: Married on Purpose

"And the Lord God commanded the man, saying, Of every tree of the garden thou mayest freely eat: But of the tree of the knowledge of good and evil, thou shalt not eat of it: for in the day that thou eatest thereof thou shalt surely die. And the Lord God said, It is not good that the man should be alone; I will make him an help meet for him."

Genesis 2:16-18 KJV

Every individual contemplating marriage may want to consider getting married with a godly purpose. Genesis chapter 2 talks about man (Adam) being put in the garden to work it. When God saw it was not good for Adam to be alone, he made a helper compatible to him. The two of them were to share in the work and dominate the earth together *(Genesis 2:16-18).* God did not intend for the man and woman to dominate each other. Man and woman were created to dominate the earth...together.

After receiving the blessing of a potential spouse, be prayerful about the thin line between a mate who is truly considerate and one who plans to dominate or control you. Women are encouraged to obey the word of God and submit to their husbands.

"Wives, submit to your own husbands, as to the Lord:" (Ephesians 5:22)

This act of submission does not mean he is to dominate you. The Greek definition of the word submit includes but is not limited to "arrange under" or "to subject one's self." It was the Greek military term meaning, "to arrange in a military fashion under the command of a leader." In non-military use, submission means "a voluntary attitude of giving in, cooperating, assuming responsibility, and carrying a burden." In laymen's terms, submit means "to fit". As you fit into your husband's plan, God graciously escorts you to your own expected end to complete your God given assignment.

Fitting in...

What does all of this mean? It means God has a plan. _"For I know the thoughts that I think toward you, saith the Lord, thoughts of peace, and not of evil, to give you an expected end." (Jeremiah 29:11 KJV)_ As you focus on fitting into your husband's plans, know God is also focusing on you. You have an assignment as well. You will arrive at the expected end He has purposed for you.

There is a plan for you and there is a plan for your mate. What you should both know is that you are not to compete. The only adversary you have is satan. Do not fall into his plan or pit to have you compete against your mate. The fight is not against flesh and blood, especially your own blood. There is so much work in the kingdom for the both of you to complete. Stay focus on "out loving" one another. This will be a plus for your marriage. Instead of focusing on "what he has done for you lately." Focus on acting out your love for him. Love is an action word. When you truly love, you act out this emotion in a positive manner. Because God so loved the world, He gave the most important gift He had, His son. Think about what you have given away lately to prove your love? What have you received from your spouse that would prove his love?

Ways to Fit in

1. Pray for wisdom concerning what God has called your husband to do as well as yourself.
2. Encourage (not nag or manipulate) your husband in his purpose.
3. Purchase self-help books for him, if he likes to read or CDs should he rather listen to subject matters that are applicable to his call.
4. Pray God sends him a godly mentor he accepts.
5. Pray for him to walk in Son-ship with God.

<u>Son-ship...</u>

Living Testimony:

During the early years of my marriage, I was victim to what most couples fall prey to in a new marriage. I was stuck focusing on his areas of improvements. I did not consider the areas I needed to correct. I was crying out to God and He did hear my cry. It appeared my requests were being boomeranged, as God spoke back informing me that I was praying in the wrong direction or amiss.

"You ask and do not receive, because you ask amiss, that you may spend it on your pleasures." (James 4:3 NKJV)

I was praying my husband would become a better husband. This type of prayer is code for "do everything I want you to do and be who I think you are supposed to be for my glory, not the glory of God." **Let's be real ladies**. The danger of this is molding him into the husband you will later, love to hate, lack respect for, and eventually fall out of love with him.

God told me, instead of praying all that nonsense; I should simply pray that my husband walks in the spirit of son-ship. This is walking in the spirit of God. As he is walking in the spirit of God, he is going to love me as Christ loves the church. Son-ship comes with the responsibility of him sanctifying, cleansing, and washing me with the word. Not from me cramming the word of God down his throat. Ouch! It is ok to be honest.

With a change of attitude and perspective, I began praying the will and word of God. Those prayers were answered. As I watched the hand of God mold my husband into becoming a son of God, I began to change. It was such a blessing to witness my husband walking in true son-ship. Ultimately, he became the husband I had hoped for, revealing the substance and evidence of what I did not see, but believed was always there!

Chapter 3: Naked and Unashamed

"And they were both naked, the man and his wife, and were not ashamed."

Genesis 2:25 KJV

Now that you have made your decision to enter into the ministry and or support your spouse in their calling, you need to take note of some important biblical truths. The first biblical truth is in the book of Genesis. When God planted Adam and Eve in the garden, they enjoyed pure fellowship with the Father. They were both naked and not ashamed.

Because of ministry challenges, it is strongly encouraged, to stay in close fellowship with the Father. It is also highly important not to be ashamed when we need guidance such as mentoring or coaching, both professionally and personally. Statistics are alarming when looking at the broken marriages of leaders in the church.

According to the Barna[5] report, 90% of Pastors report they work 55-75 hours per week. Fifty percent of Pastors report feeling unable to meet the ever-changing demands of their jobs. Seventy percent of Pastors battle depression. Fifty percent of Pastors going into the ministry will not last 5 years. Fifty percent of Pastors' marriages end in divorce. This

---

[5] https://www.barna.com/

report also states, that Seventy percent of Pastors do not have a close friend. Additionally, one more distinctive piece of information regarding threats against being in ministry as Pastors is being overweight and experiencing stress on a weekly basis. In some cases, a Pastor's physical health is noted as being worse than the average individuals in the area they live. Unfortunately, this unflattering information could go on.

The principle of these statistics are not limited to current times. The man at the pool of Bethesda claim was no one was there to put him into the water. The pool of Bethesda, having five porches, waited for those who were sick, blind, lame, and paralyzed to come. Whoever stepped in first after the waters were stirred got rid of their physical issue. A clear expectation was placed back on the individual who was in need of the healing.

> *"For an angel went down at a certain season into the pool, and troubled the water: whosoever then first after the troubling of the water stepped in was*

made whole of whatsoever disease he had. And a certain man was there, which had an infirmity thirty and eight years. When Jesus saw him lie, and knew that he had been now a long time in that case, he saith unto him, Wilt thou be made whole? The impotent man answered him, Sir, I have no man, when the water is troubled, to put me into the pool: but while I am coming, another steppeth down before me. Jesus saith unto him, Rise, take up thy bed, and walk. And immediately the man was made whole, and took up his bed, and walked: and on the same day was the sabbath." (John 5:4-9)

Jesus places the same expectation on those who serve and love him today. As leaders, we should not expect someone to submerge us into stirring waters for our healing. We have to champion our personal "self-care" if we desire to remain above reproach. We have to, at some point, become naked and unashamed. We are made of flesh and blood just like our congregation and audience. As we encourage those we lead to be honest and transparent, we too need to take a "real pill" from time to time. Leading while bleeding is not beneficial to those we serve. Bleeding is maneuvering through your mental sickness (discouragement, doubt, or unbelief) and blind to your own needs.

Emotional paralysis and a lame marriage in our home hinders our true effectiveness to the Kingdom. There is no expectation of perfection, but we need to be perfectly honest with our spouses and ourselves as we strive to mental and physical wellness.

Nicodemus was a leader in need of a leader or mentor for himself. He was a teacher that had to take time from teaching to be taught. Although Nicodemus was aware of the need for a mentor for himself, he hid the need from those around him.

> *"There was a man of the Pharisees*
> *named Nicodemus, a ruler of the*
> *Jews. This man came to Jesus by night*
> *and said to Him, 'Rabbi, we know that*
> *You are a teacher come from God; for*

no one can do these signs that You do
unless God is with him.' .... Jesus
answered and said to him, 'Are you the
teacher of Israel, and do not know these
things?'" (John 3:1-2 & 10 NKJV)

Nicodemus came to Jesus when no one could see him.
Ministers and Pastors should not have to sneak
around to receive encouragement and professional
care. Pastor forums and support groups are necessary
if you are to overcome statistics of deteriorating
health, dysfunctional marriages, and premature
deaths.

When it comes to wholeness, there is no shame in
managing our personal self-care and mental wellness.
There is no shame in voluntarily sitting one's self
down or removing one's self from teaching in order to
rest, regroup, and recharge. A self-imposed
suspension from ministering will yield a healthier you
and a healthier ministry. Without this suspension,
impurity of our thoughts and heart are inevitable.
Hebrew states, that we should rest from our work.

There remaineth therefore a rest
to the people of God. For he that
is entered into his rest, he also hath
ceased from his own works, as God
did from his. Let us labour therefore
to enter into that rest, lest any man
fall after the same example of unbelief."
(Hebrews 4:9-11 KJV)

You never just fall into sin. Falling into sin is a process
that the enemy leads you to, step-by-step. Let's be
real, when falling into sin, it actually started with a
thought lingering a little too long. The Message
version of the Bible expresses the trap of the enemy in
a slightly amusing way. While one believes sin
happens unexpectedly, it is really like getting
pregnant and having a child.

> *"The temptation to give in to evil*
> *comes from us and only us. We have*
> *no one to blame but the leering,*
> *seducing flare-up of our own lust.*
> *Lust gets pregnant, and has a baby:*
> *sin! Sin grows up to adulthood, and*

becomes a real killer." (James 1:15
MSG).

Although you feel you have great cause, your spirit will wrestle with your flesh until your flesh can be laid to rest. It is then that you will be able to allow the Holy Spirit to create in you a clean heart and renew a right spirit. When improper emotions or personal issues are not properly dealt with, you risk the possibility of preaching the negative emotions out over the entire congregation making everyone else sick.

In standing naked and unashamed, it is important not to over expose your congregation to your human frailties in the ungodly therapeutic method; I call "Emotional Cleansing through the Preached Word." As godly leaders, you should never use this method, as it is an abuse of your spiritual authority.

This emotional abuse of the congregation leaves the recipients confused and broken without a true resolution to the real issue at hand. You must learn graceful confrontation in the areas that need change.

If you never confront it properly, you cannot expect real change.

In essence, when you do not have the capacity to cast down all ungodly imaginations or thoughts, you need to voluntarily step away from the pulpit to pull yourself together. If not, you risk little sins becoming the death of you.

While you walk in being naked and not ashamed, be reminded of the old saying "check yourselves before you wreck yourselves." Those who follow Jesus are in the season of God's grace to take some time to walk away, to rest, and to be restored. You can walk away or risk God walking you away in shame.

In the event you find yourself worn-out, you must seek out some assistance. Here are a few tips to point you in the right direction.

1. Pray God directs or connects you to a godly mentor.
2. Seek out a Pastor or Minister's support group that believes in a life of holiness without promoting condemnation and judgment.

3. Pray for and find someone to be accountable.
4. Seek professional Christian counseling should God lead you in this path. Allow the hindering thought of Christian Counseling as something that is taboo to be removed. Know that more churches are partnering with Christian counselors to assist in leading and healing their flock.

You do not have to remain sin sick, blind to your own shortcoming, and lame or paralyzed. Be open for restoration. Heed the instruction of Jesus to the paralytic, get up, take your own bed up, you can begin to walk upright again (John 5:8).

Change The Church Success Paradigm

The hurt and the pain of broken churches and Pastors does not have to be this way. It should not be this way. It is time to remove the unbiblical expectations, which have been placed on Pastors' shoulders and the ones Pastors have placed on their own shoulders. Pastors were never meant to carry this big a burden. No one person is capable of being the preacher, teacher, vision-caster, CEO, leader, evangelist, soul-winner, fundraiser, marriage counselor, and all-around model of virtue most people expect Pastors to pull off. Many of the Pastors are expected to do this while working a full-time job outside the church walls. It has been done this way for so many years. It sometimes feels like a runaway train that can't be stopped. However, it must be stopped.

Redefining Success in Ministry

No one can stop this runaway train but you, the Pastors and Ministers. You have to begin to simply say no. For some, that means saying a "godly no" to the unreasonable expectations of your church members, deacon boards, and denominational officials. But for all, it means saying no to your own unbiblical expectations of yourself. Saying no to a model built and perpetuated around a combination of our own egos and insecurities.

We are not the builders of the church, Jesus is. We are not capable of working ourselves to the bone emotionally and spiritually without something breaking inside us. We cannot keep pushing ourselves physically with too little sleep, too much food and too little exercise. We cannot keep neglecting our spouses and families while we burn the ministry candle at both ends and not expect everyone – our families, our churches, and ourselves – to pay an enormous price for it. We have to redefine what success in ministry looks like. Too many good people are being hurt as we pursue our current, unsupported version of success. Remember that we need all other parts of the Body of Christ to help us obtain success in ministry.

Ministry Success

1. Establish a Prayer team to cover the leaders. Everyone faces loneliness, temptation, discouragement, and attacks but leaders often take the brunt. Esther mustered her prayer team when Haman plotted the destruction of her people (Esther 4:16). Although she was queen, she would not be exempt from Haman's evil plans. Neither would any Jew around her.

2. Continue to pray in laborers who are truly led by the spirit of God. Granting a truly God led laborer responsibilities of the ministry and access to the sheep will alleviate you from

being spread too thin. This person is to be trusted, free of selfish motives and ambition while walking in their own wholeness.

3. Beware of overzealous laborers with selfish motives and lofty ambitions. They are likely to move ahead of God promoting themselves and deceiving your sheep resulting in a church split.

4. Schedule time away from the ministry. If the ministry and vision is from God, it will continue to accomplish what God intends. If it cannot function or thrive without you, one would question if it is from God.

Pray for Each Other

It is no secret that effective ministry is challenging. Being in the business of developing people spiritually is better attempted with divine intervention. It is no simple feat that should be attempted in one's own strength. If you are serious about God and his people, it is imperative that you have a strong and consistent prayer life and time of study.

Consider the following needs of Pastors and Ministers when you pray (spoken by Karl Vaters, in Life Letter Café). "Today, let's pause. Take a breath. And pray. Pray for the hurting Pastors, known and unknown, who have left a church they loved and maybe still love. Pray for the famous Pastors suffering under the unbearable glare of the spotlight. Pray for the unknown Pastors feeling lost and forgotten. Pray for their families who have borne years of pain silently and who are bearing even more right now. Pray for the church members who don't know whether to feel angry or sad. Pray that the God who promised that his yoke was easy and his burden light, will ease the much heavier burdens we have placed on our own shoulders. And replace it with his peace, his comfort and his hope."[6]

---

[6] Karl Vaters, Life Letter Café-Encouragement for Life, September 20, 2016.

Chapter 4: Fishers of Men

"There are two types of fisherman, those who fish for sport and those who fish for fish."

Unknown Author

As you fish for men to increase the Kingdom of God, what kind of fisherman are you? Do you witness to satisfy some heavenly quota or are you really concerned about those individuals who are facing an eternal damnation? Are you fishing for men because that is what "church folk" are supposed to do or are you looking to God (not yourself) to change the life of the unbeliever?

Have you been fishing in error? Is your technique all wrong? Fishing is a process and the fish may not come in the way we think they should. You have your own unique experience of being brought into the Body of Christ. Listen to what John says,

> *"Beloved, now we are children of God; and it has not yet been revealed what we shall be, but we know that when He is revealed, we shall be like Him, for we shall see Him as He is." (John 3:2 KJV)*

Becoming like Christ is a process and takes time. It does not immediately happen once you decided to step on the church grounds or walk through the church doors. Newly retired Pete Wilson of Cross

Point Church in Nashville Tennessee stated, he cultivated an environment where the "fish" he caught could fit in before they necessarily believed. He also stated his church community was a place "where everyone is welcomed, because nobody is perfect but anything is possible". When fishing, you have to make sure your "bait" is the pure Word of God providing a gospel that is centered around God and not man. If the bait of the gospel is weak, the fish will temporarily nibble and later release the bait and move on to the next fishing establishment.

> *"And I, if I be lifted up from the earth, will draw all men unto me." (John 12:32 KJV)*

Let's compare cleaning fish in the natural with the process of fishing for men and cleaning them up. Do not skip this process; you do not want to miss the revelation of why Jesus used this imagery.

> *"Then He said to them, 'Follow Me, and I will make you fishers of men.'"* (Matthew 4:19 NKJV)

Natural Process of Cleaning Fish

1. After catching the fish, **cover the work area** with plenty of newspaper or heavy paper bags.
   a. Have a plastic bag on hand for the guts, bones, etc.
   b. Seal them well before disposing.
2. **Prepare the body**-First wash the fish in cool running water to remove any slime. With a sharp knife cut off the pectoral fins on both sides of the fish. If necessary, remove the scales with a blunt knife across the entire body.
3. **Gut the fish**-Remove the guts from the cavity. With the spoon, scoop out the dark reddish-brown kidney line that lies along the backbone.
   Important: Cut out all parts of the gills.
4. **Remove head and tail**-Cut the head off right below the gills. Cut the tail where it joins the body.
5. **Remove the dorsal fin and bones**–Do this by giving a quick pull from tail end to head. This step is not essential but eliminates those tiny, annoying bones that can ruin a meal.

Spiritual Process of Cleaning Fish

1. After "catching" or receiving an unbeliever, **cover the work area** with plenty of biblical teaching, prayer, and heavy intercession.
   a. Have a well-trained deliverance team on hand, in the event deliverance of an individual is needed.
   b. Seal this team with much prayer and training before they are released to minister. Anxious overzealous workers can pose a problem to the ministry and damage individuals.
2. **Prepare the body**–Educate the church body so they are better prepared to receive the fish. Fish come in all shapes and sizes. Some have been pierced while others have been colorfully tattooed to express their triumphs and victories. Some may know how to swim and navigate their way through church, while others may have minimal or no experience at all in navigation. Some fish may show up smelling of tobacco, marijuana, and strong drink. Some fish may be well dressed or not dressed at all. Some fish could possibly arrive to

your "ark of safety" addicted to what was familiar and available in their surroundings looking for freedom or recently freed.

3. **Gut the fish**–Fisherman, before you attempt to gut the fish, you will need the Holy Spirit's assistance. If not, you may damage the entire fish.

4. **Remove head and tail**–A good fisherman assist with cutting the head of fish off with the purpose of the new fish getting a renewed mind with the things of God. The tail of the fish is the device that serves as a rudder of sorts guiding the fish to various destinations. If you encourage the fish to renew its mind, it does not want to do the things it once did and go to the places it once went.

5. **Remove the dorsal fin and bones**–The dorsal fin is used to balance the fish. Once you become citizens of the Kingdom, the Holy Spirit becomes your Comforter and your Guide. Encourage the fish or new convert to develop a personal relationship with the Holy Spirit. Instruct them to listen for His voice and not just yours. Remember this: "However, when He, the Spirit of truth, has come, He will guide you into all truth; for He will

not speak on His own authority, but whatever He hears He will speak; and He will tell you things to come." (John 16:13 NKJV) As for the bones, no one is without a skeleton in the closet from which they need to free themselves. Extend this grace to one another.

When appointing others to assist you in mentoring the flock, get to know those who you appoint. Discern their motives and intentions before releasing them to mentor others in the church. Spiritual mentors should refrain from trying to become Holy Ghost to the people of God.

When mentoring new converts, make sure you are also striving for your own personal wholeness as well. It is not possible to mentor others out of your own brokenness. Oftentimes a broken person's sole purpose is to keep the new convert dependent on them to satisfy their need to be wanted and in some cases needed. The spirit of brokenness attracts more brokenness, which has posed a problem in the Body of Christ. In addition, hurting people continue to hurt people, but "healed people heal people."[7]

---

[7] Demetrica Michelle M., Healing the Family Ministries.

Chapter 5: Deep Sea Fishing

Matthew 13:24-30 NKJV

Now you are ready to go deep-sea fishing! Refer to the Parable of the Sower.

"24 Another parable He put forth to them, saying: "The kingdom of heaven is like a man who sowed good seed in his field;

25 but while men slept, his enemy came and sowed tares among the wheat and went his way.

26 But when the grain had sprouted and produced a crop, then the tares also appeared.

27 So the servants of the owner came and said to him, 'Sir, did you not sow good seed in your field? How then does it have tares?'

28 He said to them, 'An enemy has done this.' The servants said to him, 'Do you want us then to go and gather them up?'

29 But he said, 'No, lest while you gather up the tares you also uproot the wheat with them.

30 Let both grow together until the harvest, and at the time of harvest I will say to the reapers, "First gather together the tares and bind them in bundles to burn them, but gather the wheat into my barn.""

Look closer at this familiar text. Perhaps you have been taught the one who sowed the good seed is the Son of Man. The field represents the world and the good seeds are Children of the Kingdom. Most commentaries teach the tares are children of the wicked one, the enemy who sowed them is the devil, the harvest is end of world, and the reapers are the angels who gathered the tares to burn them in the fire. However, there is a much deeper revelation to this parable. To gain a better understanding of this parable, here are some agriculture facts concerning the wheat and the tare.

The early stages of a wheat plant and a tare plant look extremely similar.

The Wheat:

- The wheat plant has substance and bears grain that causes it to bow from the weight.

- The bowing over of the wheat plant is symbolic to the humility the people of God should possess. The wheat plant gives life and is one of the main substance in most food products.

The Tare:

- The tare looks exactly like the wheat. In fact, it is actually a degenerative wheat, meaning something has caused it to change itself to a lower dysfunctional form of the wheat.

- When the tare starts growing up, it actually begins to change its form and becomes a lighter substance standing straight up bearing only microscopic poisonous seeds.

- Eating these poisonous seeds cause dizziness, nausea, and sickness. The tare plant kills instead of giving life.

- The wheat and tare plants start out indistinguishable; the only way to tell the difference is when the two come into maturity.

- Separating the wheat and the tare at harvest time keep the deadly consequences at bay.

Agriculturally speaking, both the wheat and the tare share the same root. When something shares the same root, issues arise when it is time to separate the two. The book of Matthew 13: 24 states, "Another parable He put forth to them, saying: "The Kingdom of heaven is like a man who sowed good seed in his field;"[8] Taking some theological freedom here to imagine, perhaps the man is God the Creator. God the Creator takes this good seed and sows it into your Mother's Womb.

> *"For You formed my innermost parts; You knit me [together] in my mother's womb. I will give thanks and praise to You, for I am fearfully and wonderfully made;"(Psalms 139:13-14 Amplified)*

---

[8] New King James Version

As a child of God, you become the field. You are created in the image of a Holy God. Each field is "fearfully and wonderfully made." In this field, the creator places a divine destiny carefully knitting it together with a purpose and calling. Each field is a designer's original.

After designing this field and planning well for it, the Creator took a rest, allowing men to keep the field. The parable also tells you man slept. The statement "while men slept" is not necessarily referring to physical sleep. People sometimes take on a sense of *unconsciousness* in the form of slothfulness, laziness, indifference, uncaring, unresponsiveness, and even being unsympathetic. This state of sleep translates biblically to mean man is yielding to their own sin and are not following the ways of God. This time of sleeping could have happened during your youth or parenting years. During the time you are supposed to be parenting or being parented, the enemy comes in to sow tares in your life, stunt your growth or perhaps choke out your purpose in God.

For example, when you are too young to know better, the enemy unleashes perversion to use in the forms of childhood bullying, physical or verbal abuse, sexual molestation or early addictions and arrested development. The tares of bullying and verbal abuse may come from the way a person looks, poverty, skin color or aptitude, which has a tendency to damage a person's self-esteem and identity.

The tares of sexual molestation introduce sexual promiscuity, sexual perversion, same sex attraction struggles and homosexuality. The tare of addiction can last a lifetime posing challenges and bondage that hinders a person from walking in the freedom for which God has made them free.

Some people may have experienced rejection from their parents at birth and subjected to the tormenting rejection whispers from the enemy. In many cases, those who are parenting are not paying close enough attention to provide protection, when these tares are being sowed. Regardless of the *tare tactic* the enemy uses, it can be detrimental to a person as they strive to become whom God made them.

Matthew goes on to tell what happens to the wheat and the tare, *"26But when the grain had sprouted and produced a crop, then the tares also appeared.* Now, you have a beautifully woven piece of art, carefully knitted, and created by God. During the appointed time that the wheat is to sprout, be productive, and began to walk out its true purpose, the tares become a hindrance. Remember, Man is a tri-being, who has a spirit, soul, and physical body, which work together. Damages to the physical body, brings damage to the spirit. When something is off in your spirit, your flesh has a propensity to attempt to mask or cover it up.

One biblical example of the effects of tares on a tri-being is demonstrated in Genesis when Adam and Eve encountered the serpent. Adam and Eve sensed something was spiritually off. The Bible says in Genesis 3:7, *"Then the eyes of both of them were opened, and they knew that they were naked; and they sewed fig leaves together and made themselves coverings."*

Instead of coming clean with God, they found fig leaves as they attempted to mask or cover up their disobedience. When tares show up in your life, you must know that you have to press pass these intentional productivity blockers, illegitimate roadblocks and strive to become the people God intended. It never sits well with God when the enemy sow tares and influence God's people into believing they are not who God created them to be.

In the Garden of Eden, God poses the question "Who told you, you were naked?" God poses this question for you today, when you attempt to mask your tares, taking the wrong path never becoming the person God intends you to be. Who told you, you were ugly? Who told you, you are not anointed? Who told you, you were too dark, too dumb, too fat, too tall, or too short? If it did not come from God, it is a lie from the "father of lies".

The servants of the owner of the field come to the owner to clarify what had been planted in the field. (Matthew 13:27)

Theological freedom, imagine the servants are God-sent School Teachers, Coaches, Parents or Pastors. They become concerned when they see you are masked, hiding the tares. They know you have been raised with good parenting, good training, good teaching yet you continue to wear a mask and cover up who you are to be in Christ. They are perplexed at the infiltration of the tares. Where did these TARES come from? The explanation is simple and is found in Matthew 13:28.

> *"He said to them, 'An enemy has done this.' The servants said to him, 'Do you want us then to go and gather them up?'"*

A sovereign God, who created everything in the earth, including satan the deceiver, reminds man that this was not his original plan for their lives, but the plan of the enemy. As a Minister, be clear, that a simple rebuke may not set all back in its original state. In some cases, the laying on of hands on these tares, slinging oil over it, speaking in tongues or fasting and praying become counterproductive. In over zealously gathering up these tares you may uproot the wheat.

> *"But he said, 'No, lest while you gather up the tares you also uproot the wheat with them."*
> (Matthew 13:29)

In essence, you could damage and in some cases destroy the individual, making matters worse. While attempting to uproot the tare, you could injure the person's purpose. Keep in mind, while you are fishing, follow the instruction in Matthew 13:30.

> *"Let both grow together (wheat and our tares) until the harvest, and at the time of harvest I will say to the reapers, 'First gather together the tares and bind them in bundles to burn them, but gather the wheat into my barn'"* (Matthew 13:30 *paraphrased*).

The purpose is to entrust the reaping to the Holy Spirit, because He produces the purity of God in everyone's life. God's plan is to purify and the spirit is the agent of sanctification. He can fill the fish, sanctify, lead, wash it and make it new. He is totally able to regenerate and make damaged, undamaged. As the silversmith uses fire to purge the waste from the precious metal, in like manner, God uses the Spirit to remove your sin. His fire cleanses and refines the fisherman and his catch. Again, knowing the word and applying the word leads to true transformation for everyone.

Chapter 6: True Sisterhood

Numbers 27:1-11 NKJV

One of the most disturbing revelations in the study of the Bible is the truth that God placed enmity between the woman and satan. He also placed enmity between the woman's seed and satan's seed. This enmity is mishandled and influences true sisterhood.

> *"And I will put enmity between thee and the woman, and between thy seed and her seed; it shall bruise thy head, and thou shalt bruise his heel." (Genesis 3:5)*

Enmity is animosity, antagonism, friction, bitterness, resentment, ill filling, ill will, bad blood, hatred and so on. The simple biblical definition of enmity is blood feud. As a result, of mankind walking in disobedience, the death sentence includes a blood feud between the woman and the serpent as well as the seed of the woman and the serpent. Because the adversary is crafty, we have to be spiritually mature to watching how he works.

> *"Put on the whole armor of God, that you may be able to stand against the wiles of the devil." (Ephesians 6:11 NKJV)*

The word "wiles" comes from the Greek word **methodeía**, meth-od-i'-ah. Wiles means cunning arts, deceit, craft and trickery. There is often a method to his madness, involuntarily participated in when a sister harms another sister. He strategically hides behind this enmity while blood feuds against each other and not him are manifesting. Understanding this, why do women struggle to get along in and outside the church?

Why do Pastors have to waste time refereeing clicks in the church, schisms in the body of Christ, and emulations in what is supposed to be the holy place? Galatians answers this question making it crystal clear. Women have to learn how to get out of their feelings and flesh.

> *"Now the works of the flesh are manifest, which are these; Adultery, fornication, uncleanness, lasciviousness, Idolatry, witchcraft, hatred, variance, emulations, wrath, strife, seditions, heresies, Envyings, murders, drunkenness, revellings, and such like: of the which I tell you before, as I have*

also told you in time past, that they which do such things shall not inherit the kingdom of God." (Galatians 5:19-21)

Satan literally feeds off the flesh. *"...and dust shalt thou eat all the days of thy life:" (Genesis 3:14)* Humans are spirit beings formed from the dust of the earth. When man dies, the bodies (or the flesh) returns to dust. Each time man walks in the flesh or dust this is feeding the adversary.

You starve him out, by walking in the spirit. *"But the fruit of the Spirit is love, joy, peace, longsuffering, gentleness, goodness, faith, Meekness, temperance: against such there is no law (Galatians 5:22-23).* Walking more in the spirit promotes true Sisterhood.

My sisterhood experience:
Being born in a family of four sisters, we joke about being born in an actual society of sisters. Although we have very different personalities and dispositions, we all love each other and get along extremely well as we enjoy true sisterhood.

We capitalize and embrace one another's strengths while applying grace to each other's weaknesses, as we stand united in this race of life. Understanding this, one of my favorite books in the Bible concerning sisterhood is the book of Numbers chapter 27:1-11 with the daughter of Zelophehad.

> "*¹Then came the daughters of Zelophehad the son of Hepher, the son of Gilead, the son of Machir, the son of Manasseh, from the families of Manasseh the son of Joseph; and these were the names of his daughters: Mahlah, Noah, Hoglah, Milcah, and Tirzah.*
>
> *² And they stood before Moses, before Eleazar the priest, and before the leaders and all the congregation, by the doorway of the tabernacle of meeting, saying:*
>
> *³ "Our father died in the wilderness; but he was not in the company of those who gathered together against the Lord, in company with Korah, but he died in his own sin; and he had no sons.*
>
> *⁴ Why should the name of our father be removed from among his family because he had no son? Give us a possession among our father's brothers."*
>
> *⁵ So Moses brought their case before the Lord.*
>
> *⁶ And the Lord spoke to Moses, saying:*

7 "The daughters of Zelophehad speak what is right; you shall surely give them a possession of inheritance among their father's brothers, and cause the inheritance of their father to pass to them.

8 And you shall speak to the children of Israel, saying: 'If a man dies and has no son, then you shall cause his inheritance to pass to his daughter.

9 If he has no daughter, then you shall give his inheritance to his brothers.

10 If he has no brothers, then you shall give his inheritance to his father's brothers.

11 And if his father has no brothers, then you shall give his inheritance to the relative closest to him in his family, and he shall possess it.'" And it shall be to the children of Israel a statute of judgment, just as the Lord commanded Moses."

The sisters (or women), came together, devised a plan, and stood united for the same cause while overturning a statue of judgment and this is the premise of this account. One can only imagine, if the women in the Kingdom of God all came together, some of the common causes of discontent would be eliminated in the church not to mention the world. The spirit of unity displayed by these five sisters resulted in them obtaining their inheritance. There are some things that God has purposed for us to have if we would only come together in the power of unity and sisterhood.

Remember the story of the Egyptian and Hebrew women from opposite walks of life banning together, going against the orders of Pharaoh because they were filled with compassion, concerning the birth of the male babies and feared God.

> *"15 Then the king of Egypt spoke to the Hebrew midwives, of whom the name of one was Shiphrah and the name of the other Puah; 16 and he said, "When you do the duties of a midwife for the Hebrew women, and see them on the birthstools, if it is a son, then you shall kill him; but if it is a daughter, then she shall live." 17 But the midwives feared God, and did not do as the king of Egypt commanded them, but saved the male children alive. 18 So the king of Egypt called for the midwives and said to them, "Why have you done this thing, and saved the male children alive?"*

19 And the midwives said to Pharaoh, "Because the Hebrew women are not like the Egyptian women; for they are lively and give birth before the midwives come to them."

20 Therefore God dealt well with the midwives, and the people multiplied and grew very mighty. 21 And so it was, because the midwives feared God, that He provided households for them." (Exodus 1:15-20 NKJV)

At first glance, the controversy would appear to be "much to do about nothing," since the text itself states, "And the king of Egypt spoke to the Hebrew midwives," The issue is not quite as clear as it might seem. Numerous biblical scholars and commentators, who have studied the original Hebrew language within the text of Exodus 1:1-22, have concluded, in the context, the term "Hebrew midwives" actually should be interpreted as "midwives to the Hebrews". Also, note the women bear Egyptian names, and were probably Egyptian. It makes sense that Pharaoh would not have entrusted this task to the Hebrew women themselves. These Egyptian women were instructed to kill the male Hebrew babies. A united force was established between these women; great deliverance was birth from this improbable teamwork.

In essence, true sisterhood is obtainable if women get out of their own way. How do we promote true Sisterhood?

As Pastors and Ministers, you need to remind yourself and each other of the following truths:

1. Continue to hope and pray that the love of God is shed abroad in the hearts of all women. *"And hope maketh not ashamed; because the love of God is shed abroad in our hearts by the Holy Ghost which is given unto us"* (Romans 5:5).

2. Know your sister is not the enemy. She is your mid-wife and will be useful during your birthing process. How many women have died attempting to give birth all alone? How many midwives withheld their gifts and watched sisters die and that which she was to give birth to dies with her? Everyone is pregnant with dreams and aspirations. What women are birthing will come in all sizes and functions. Women can celebrate each other without having to compare what each is carrying.

Women can carry their promises together without competing for attention. Mary and Elizabeth demonstrates this unifying relationship. One carrying the forerunner, John and the other carrying Jesus, the Christ. Mary did not exalt her pregnancy over Elizabeth's pregnancy. Elizabeth did not feel inferior to Mary. They were both happy to be pregnant with promise.

3. *"For we wrestle not against flesh and blood, but against principalities, against powers, against the rulers of the darkness of this world, against spiritual wickedness in high places."*[9] Nowhere in this verse does it say we are to wrestle with each other.

4. Believe and know that women are better together and should strive for this unity. Take courage to correct other sisters when they are spreading discord.

5. Refrain from gossip. This is an important point to take note. When someone says something to you about another sister and it is clearly at ill

will, ask the deliverer of the gossip if the two of you can discuss what was said. Gossip only dies when we kill it. If you are always the church dumpster for gossip, search yourself.

6. Continue to plan social, community service events, outings and retreats so the women can really get to know one another outside of the church walls.

Chapter 7: Ruling Your Own House

I Timothy 3:1-5 NKJV

The following maybe a familiar quote you have heard often.

> *"This is a faithful saying: If a man*
> *desires the position of a bishop,[a] he*
> *desires a good work. 2 A bishop then*
> *must be blameless, the husband of one*
> *wife, temperate, sober-minded, of good*
> *behavior, hospitable, able to teach; 3 not*
> *given to wine, not violent, not greedy*
> *for money, [b] but gentle, not*
> *quarrelsome, not covetous; 4 one who*
> *rules his own house well,*
> *having his children in submission with*
> *all reverence 5 (for if a man does not*
> *know how to rule his own house, how*
> *will he take care of the church of God?"*

The operative word here is "own house". The congregation and community often scrutinizes children of Pastors as well as their own parents, yes their own parents. Pastors and Ministers who are parents make a covenant to raise their children in ministry in a way that they would never be in the position to make an accusation against God, their parents, or the church. In order to do this, family has to come first.

This goal of balancing family life and kingdom service is actually included in the Vision Statement at Kingdom Family International Church. Frequent church attendance has nothing to do with a pure relationship with God. You can be in the church every time the church doors open but until the spirit of God settles in your spirit and rule over your flesh, you are only increasing frequent attendance points in the earth and not in the kingdom. The quality of time spent in the house of God is more important than the quantity of time spent. Dragging your children to church does not make them any more save than dragging a shopping cart into a department store make you a big spender. When there is an imbalance in the home, children tend to stray away from the faith and leave a trail of accusations against God, parents, and the church.

How to accusation-proof your children in ministry

1. Encourage your children to involve themselves in wholesome activities outside of church and the ministry.
2. Make sure you or your spouse support their activities.
3. Encourage the parents of your ministry to support their children without feeling guilty of occasionally missing church events.
4. Make sure you take family vacations that are void of church talk in their presence.
5. When attending college or becoming an adult, release them from attending your ministry. Kindly suggest visiting another ministry with your child if they feel God is calling them to another ministry. Do this properly so you can release them properly emotionally and spiritually.

Pastors with children, your goal should be consistent with every other God fearing parent. You should simply raise your children in the nurture and admonition of the Lord.[10] Training them in the way they should go is an expectation for all parents' not just preachers with children.[11] While living in your house or under your roof, expect your children to govern themselves in the way of the Lord. The word is not short on reminding parents to discipline your children.

However, the truth of the matter is you cannot control the will of another. You can influence them with the consequences such as rod of correction, revoked privileges, and godly precepts by living a life upright before them. You must understand, you can do all of this and they can still follow their ungodly will and the way of the world.

The word never guarantees they will not stray. The only guarantee is they will not fully depart from it. Proper teaching is downloaded in their spirit man in a reserve tank to be access when they decide to reconcile themselves back to God.

---

[10] Ephesians 6:4
[11] Proverbs 22:6

Chapter 8: It's Not Always Personal

"The stone which the builders rejected
Has become the chief cornerstone."
Psalm 118:22 NKJV

As a carrier of the gospel, like Jesus, you will need to become accustomed to rejection. Jesus was rejected on all sorts of levels. How can you attempt to build without the chief cornerstone?

In ancient building practices, the cornerstone was the principal stone placed at the corner of the structure. The cornerstone was not only the largest but was the most solid and skillfully placed stone of all the stones placed in the structure. Jesus is described as the cornerstone, in which His church would be built upon; a unified body of believers for all mankind. In the end, He Himself was rejected.

After the massive healings, feedings, and deliverances, toward the end of his life, Jesus was rejected. As Pastors, do not lose heart when God allows you to minister healing to the people, feed them spiritual and physical food, and minister deliverance, all to witness them walk away from the ministry. Just remind yourself of Jesus' rejection and do not take it personal. This does not negate the fact that Pastors and Ministers do make mistakes and experience some missteps resulting in the people walking away in offense and yes obedience to the voice of God. Jesus was perfect in all His ways and they rejected him. It is not always personal. People are people with personal needs that your ministry may or may not always meet. Individuals who feel handcuffed, desiring to leave the ministry are reckless as they look for opportunities to wreak much havoc during the remainder of their tenure in the ministry. Dr. Tony Evans describes them as a cancer that may need to be cut away from the body decreasing the chance of the disease of dissatisfaction within the ministry spreading.

How to manage a dissatisfied congregant.

1. Watch for the signs of congregational restlessness:
    a. Increase in tardiness and absenteeism
    b. Resignation from ministry posts
    c. Avoidance and additional absenteeism
2. Schedule a meeting with the congregant that seems somewhat restless.
3. Listen to their concerns to determine validity.
4. Make suggested changes if led by God.
5. When concerns are not valid, pray for the congregant.

6. Encourage them to follow church protocol in the event the restlessness continues and they feel like "their season is over".

7. Encourage them to arrange a godly departure from the ministry. In the event they fail to follow protocol, as most do, release them to God as you bid a blessed farewell.

Initially, this was a challenge for me because I did not want someone to leave offended and evangelizing on the topic of "church hurt". This is not a good look for the kingdom of God. It hinders the unsaved and the disenfranchised (those who were once saved) from attending church.

My husband would often encourage me saying, the sheep we are called to shepherd are ultimately God's people. God allows them to come and go from your church to the next church, as they will. Jesus continued to stay focus on his assignment and we should too.

I finally begin to walk in that level of release and freedom during my quiet time with God when I came across the following passage of scripture:

"Thus says the Lord: "A voice is heard in Ramah, Lamentation and bitter weeping, Rachel is weeping for her children, Refusing to be comforted for her children, because they are no more." Thus says the Lord: "Keep your voice from weeping, and your eyes from tears; for your work shall be rewarded, says the Lord:" (Jeremiah 31:15-16 NKJV)

Strive to keep your heart pure. Lace bouts of frustration with much prayer and faith so the people will not keep you from entering into your personal promise land. This happened to Moses; do not allow it to happen to you.

Chapter 9: Your Gift(s)

I Corinthians 12:4-31 NKJV

Whether you are a Pastor or a Pastor's wife, you should know you have at least one spiritual gift. Growing up in a traditional church setting, we were not exposed to spiritual gifts. We only saw the gift of preaching and singing. I was a college student attending United Student Fellowship at North Carolina State University before I was exposed to teaching on spiritual gifts.

When you are ignorant to your spiritual gifts and what God has called you to do, you become an emotional wreck. If not an emotional wreck, you settle in areas God never intended you to settle. If you are to be productive fruit bearing individuals, you have to complete a self-awareness exercise of your gifts. When you do know who you are in Christ, do not risk the possibility of allowing people to tell you any different. You will be unaware of individuals' motives; however, you can surely trust the Holy Spirit to lead you to all truth. Do not down play your spiritual gift. All gifts are needed for the Body of Christ.

What are spiritual gifts? Paul tells of the many gifts and their different functions in I Corinthians.

"4 There are diversities of gifts, but the same Spirit.

5 There are differences of ministries, but the same Lord.

6 And there are diversities of activities, but it is the same God who works all in all.

7 But the manifestation of the Spirit is given to each one for the profit of all:

8 for to one is given the word of wisdom through the Spirit, to another the word of knowledge through the same Spirit,

9 to another faith by the same Spirit, to another gifts of healings by the same[b] Spirit,

10 to another the working of miracles, to another prophecy, to another discerning of spirits, to another different *kinds of tongues, to another the interpretation of tongues.*

11 But one and the same Spirit works all these things, distributing to each one individually as He wills.

12 For as the body is one and has many members, but all the members of that one body, being many, are one body, so also is Christ.

13 For by one Spirit we were all baptized into one body—whether Jews or Greeks, whether slaves or free—and have all been made to drink into[c] one Spirit.

14 For in fact the body is not one member but many." (I Corinthians 12:4-14)

How do I determine what my spiritual gift is?

1. Pray and ask God for what purpose did He create you.

2. Take the spiritual gift test. There are several online.

3. Ask someone you trust to discuss your results with you.

4. In the spirit of decency and order, begin to slowly test drive your gifts. For example, to test drive my gift of prophecy, while attending an event were the gift of prophecy was flowing, I would pray and listen to God. I would then listen to the prophet to see if I hear them say what God has said to me about a person. What I was looking for is agreement in the spirit between the prophet who was speaking and me.

5. After determining your gift, find someone who flows in the same gift to mentor you.

Do not minimize your spiritual gifting. Whatever you are called to do matters to the gift giver. Do not compare your gift with others.

"15 If the foot should say, "Because I am not a hand, I am not of the body," is it therefore not of the body?

16 And if the ear should say, "Because I am not an eye, I am not of the body," is it therefore not of the body?

17 If the whole body were an eye, where would be the hearing? If the whole were hearing, where would be the smelling?

18 But now God has set the members, each one of them, in the body just as He pleased.

19 And if they were all one member, where would the body be?

20 But now indeed there are many members, yet one body.

21 And the eye cannot say to the hand, "I have no need of you"; nor again the head to the feet, "I have no need of you."

²² No, much rather, those members of the body which seem to be weaker are necessary.

²³ And those members of the body which we think to be less honorable, on these we bestow greater honor; and our unpresentable parts have greater modesty,

²⁴ but our presentable parts have no need. But God composed the body, having given greater honor to that part which lacks it,

²⁵ that there should be no schism in the body, but that the members should have the same care for one another.

²⁶ And if one member suffers, all the members suffer with it; or if one member is honored, all the members rejoice with it." (I Corinthians 12:15-26)

On the other hand, do not maximize your gift.

"27 Now you are the body of Christ, and members individually.

28 And God has appointed these in the church: first apostles, second prophets, third teachers, after that miracles, then gifts of healings, helps, administrations, varieties of tongues.

29 Are all apostles? Are all prophets? Are all teachers? Are all workers of miracles?

30 Do all have gifts of healings? Do all speak with tongues? Do all interpret?

31 But earnestly desire the best[d] gifts. And yet I show you a more excellent way."

Stay humble and resist the spirit of pride. In other words, do not start drinking your own Kool-Aid. To staying humble and resisting pride became a covenant that my husband and I made with each other. (I Corinthians 12:27-31)

Chapter 10: The Weapon of Mass Distractions

"Distractions are illegitimate roadblocks."

One of the largest struggles for me personally was getting past distractions. While in a Masterclass with Dr. Saundra Williams, my "aha" moment came when I came face to face with my own truth. I was standing in my own way. I was allowing distractions to hinder me from being productive in the Kingdom of God. It was then that the Holy Spirit spoke to me and said, *"Distractions are illegitimate roadblocks"* in our lives. He instructed me to keep moving when they manifested themselves in my life. I had a peaceful childhood and became accustomed to residing in a kumbaya environment. At my core and in my heart of hearts, I simply want everyone to be happy (boy am I in the wrong profession). Ministerial discord is like the waves of the oceans. They will consistently present themselves in the game of life in a gentle way.

As mighty women of God, we have to master being able to make the necessary adjustments when needed. I had to remind myself, I am not wrestling against flesh and blood. I am in a fight *"against rulers, authorities, cosmic powers of this present darkness, against spiritual forces of evil in the heavenly places."* (Ephesians 6:12 NRSV) Here is my recommendation, keep your eyes off the people and keep them fixed on the author and finisher of your faith.

Continue to look to the hills from where our help comes from. Remind yourself that He that began a good work in you will complete it until the day of Jesus Christ.

The enemy will send distractions in all shapes and sizes. They come wrapped in beautiful packages and good intentions.

Distraction is the weapon of mass destruction form by the devil. However, you can rest in the fact that no weapon that is formed against you will prosper.[12] Distractions keep you from being the student. Pastors are students too. This is confirmed in the story of Mary and Martha. Mary has taken a seat at the feet of Jesus. Martha focused on tending to household duties. This symbolizes the fundamental decision that Mary has made for her life.

---

[12] Isaiah 54:17

To take the position of sitting at someone's feet was an expression in Jesus' day that indicated the relationship between the disciple and rabbi or student and teacher. For example, Saul of Tarsus sat at the feet of Gamaliel (Acts 22:3). Saul of Tarsus was listening and learning as he focused on the words of his teacher. To sit at someone's feet meant to be their student, protégé, or mentee. Distractions, such as Facebook, watching television and cleaning out all that senseless email from advertisers hinder you from taking the time to sit at the feet of Jesus. You cannot be "sitting at his feet" and doing all the other things just mentioned. In the opinion of many, there is no such thing as multitasking. You need to learn how to be with God and only Him in those moments.

Although Mary's sister Martha is working in the kitchen. The gospel writer Luke does not say she was over-committed; he uses the word cumbered or distracted. Distracted means to be physically pulled or dragged away from something.

What are you allowing to physically pull or drag you from God and the things of God? Sometimes it can be an obsession with your adult children. With adult children, you can inundate yourselves making plans for their lives instead of trusting God to lead and guide them. Family can unknowingly be used to distract you when they have little to no direction for their own lives. The busyness of ministry is a major distraction. Delegate, delegate, and delegate! Whatever the weapon of distraction is, disarm it and focus on God and the things of God. Good intentions are not necessarily God intentions.

How to remain focus

1. Get organize and plan your day. "You have to plan to be successful" (Dr. Saundra William-the Vision Building Institute for Women).
2. Carve out quite time & study time with God.
3. Establish realistic expectations for yourself and the congregation.
4. Have goal buddies or accountability partners.
5. Have a self-reward program when completing large goals.

Chapter 11: Overcoming Your Critics

"Don't criticize what you can't understand."

Bob Dylan, Song Writer

If you would take the advice of Bob Dylan (quoted above), the church would be a much peaceable and productive place. Not only would it benefit the modern church, but it would have been profitable for the church in Jesus' day.

The Sadducees and the Pharisees were religious parties in Jesus' day. Both were critical of and were criticized by Jesus. Jesus was qualified to be critical of them because He understood what they were trying to do.

However, from their perspective, because they did not understand Jesus' assignment they spent the majority of their time criticizing Him. Many of your critics will do the same.

The Sadducees thought of themselves as "conservatives", as the Old Believers. They accepted only the written Law of Moses as the authoritative law and rejected subsequent revelation. As a result, the Sadducees denied many of the doctrines held by the Pharisees and by Jesus, including the resurrection of the dead, the existence of angels and spirits, and the meting out of rewards and punishment after death.

Contrariwise, the Pharisees were a lay group more representative of the common man. In addition to the written Law of Moses, the Pharisees accepted as authoritative principles, the rest of what is known today as the Old Testament, and the "tradition of the elders". They opposed Jesus because they did not understand the work of the Holy Spirit. The Pharisees did not understand the truth spoken by Jesus. Furthermore, they did not understand Jesus. Since they had never seen Jesus, and had never been in the company of Jesus, they made the mistake being one of many vocal critics of Jesus. How joyful it would be it our critics would pray for some understanding to accompany their wisdom.

> *"Wisdom is the principal thing; therefore get wisdom: and with all thy getting get understanding." (Proverbs 4:7 KJV)*

Beware, there will be seasons of having to bear criticisms from unqualified critics. During this time, be sure to spend it clinging to the altar in much prayer. The most challenging aspect of this season is watching the spirit of common day Pharisees and

Sadducees come together for one common goal, to oppose you.

In a conversation with a fellow First Lady, she termed this bizarre relationship with your critics as "Triangularism". Triangularism is witnessing those who are archenemies putting their differences aside to come against you. Like the Sadducees and Pharisees in Jesus day, people who were once on the opposite end of a spiritual spectrum, now combine their forces to distract, discourage and disband your purpose in God.

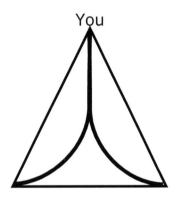

This divisive spirit means you no good with its trappings of discord and confusion. Remain silent when confronted to avoid your part in the upcoming conversations when the opposing teams link up. It is a set up to discredit you by your critics.

If you are a sitting First Lady, take your rightful place next to your husband. Regardless of the spiritual gift distribution, you are the only one qualified to stand by him. Let it be known that there is no need for any competing in this position. Not only should this point be a visual to the congregation but it needs to be spoken by the man whose side you stand and by the man who is propped up by your prayers. Yes, be grateful for the ones who cheer him on, but take your place as his head cheerleader.

Chapter 12: Count me in

James 1:2-4 NKJV

Ministry has its highs and lows; this you know or will know soon enough. You learn to carefully celebrate the triumphs and pray through the defeats. If God has called you to ministry, make up your mind that you will *count it all joy.*

I occasionally fantasize about what life would be like without all the incoming and outgoing calls, ministry appointments, visits to the hospitals, study and prep times, supporting other ministries, constant church attendance to Bible Study, intercessory prayer and regularly scheduled worship services. My, how different would life be if you could wake up on a rainy Sunday and decide to sleep in? Let's not mention the freedom to be able to occasionally answer your mockers and accusers, although Jesus never did. These few seconds, I periodically entertain result in the casting down of the imaginations and these particular fantasies that temporarily exalted itself against the knowledge of God.[13] Everyone has to bring into captivity every thought to the obedience of Christ (even me). After pinching myself I begin my self-talk spill about how I am chosen to carry the Gospel of

---

[13] II Corinthians 10:5

Jesus Christ and snatch people out of hell. The realities of life definitely set in the awesome call of God to lead the lost to him.

James 1:2-4 has become my mantra as I have persevered through some challenging seasons of ministry.

> *"My brethren, count it all joy when you fall into various trials, 3 knowing that the testing of your faith produces patience. 4 But let patience have its perfect work, that you may be perfect and complete, lacking nothing."*

What is James really saying? Here is my interpretation: Kingdom citizens, command and take authority when life happens or in life circumstances, whatever it is, be joyfully glad as soon as you encounter it, regardless of the source or root, remember your integrity is on the line. Your faithfulness and devotion to God is being observed. Come to know this test will prove to you and others what you really believe about God. As a result, you will learn perseverance, steadfastness, consistency which makes you mature and in the likeness of Christ.

Know this; you pass through life one time and one time only. Passing through time from eternity and back to eternity again only happens once, although we live in the age where the concept of recycling is apparent. Understanding this, it is important to maximize this time and minimize the distractions (or gnats) of life. It is often the small things one allows to kill, steal, and destroy the joys of life.

Be clear in your understanding that you have no control over people and their actions. People will show you who they really are, you have to accept it and continue to stay focused on the things God has called you to do. You are to stand in a place of being a grace extender, whether it is extended back to you or not.
Remember, "People are God's people and He allows them to come and go as they please". When you are told by "the people" that their season is up in your ministries, count it all joy, bid them a blessed farewell and focus on those who are left to assist you with carrying out the mission and vision God has given

you. Revelations 3:2 says it best *"and strengthen the things which remain"*.

It is a challenge to see people you love leave (it was for me). It literally stings when those you had nurtured, fed naturally and physically, and held their hands during the death of a loved one, would choose to walk in the spirit of offense and leave the ministry. You must learn it comes with the territory. You have to take God at his word when He says, *"And we know that all things work together for good to them that love God, to them who are the called according to his purpose."* (Romans 8:28)

This passage of scripture is my lifeline to staying in the race. There were days when things did not look good and days when I did not like what God was allowing to happen. It was during this time, my faith and confidence in Him grew.

As people come and go, God will always sustain the ministry and continued with His work. One of our leaders would often state, *"God will do his work with or without us"*. This proved to be true. Even as

Pastors and Leaders, you need to know that this statement is true. No one is indispensable in the kingdom of God. Yes, not even you.

You must remain prayerful and instructed by God on meeting the needs of the flock. There may be legitimate reasons why people leave your ministries and you should be concerned and make the necessary changes when possible, to avoid this continuing to happen.

Remember, *"that the race is not to the swift, nor the battle to the strong, neither yet bread to the wise, nor yet riches to men of understanding, nor yet favour to men of skill; but time and chance happeneth to them all."* (Ecclesiastes 9:11)

Since time and chance happens to us all, sacrifice your time in the earth for a gracious God and take the chance to feed his sheep. And as you do it, count it all joy!

10 Commandments of a Clergy's Wife

1. **Have a Secret Place**
   - Time in prayer and personal study is vital to your spiritual survival and sanity.
   - Do not let the busyness of ministry hijack this time with God.

2. **Remember Who You Are**
   - Your Identity is not tied to what you do; it is who you are at your core.
   - Being a Pastor's wife is one of the many roles you play.
   - The person you really are is to be cultivated outside this role.

3. **Love The Man You Married**
   - It is quite cumbersome to respect and support a man you really are not in love with. Fervently pray that God allows you to fall in love again.

- The respect will follow and supporting him will no longer be a challenge.

4. **Live a Balanced Life**

- Make sure that you maintain a life outside of the call of ministry.
- Cultivate friendships that are not connected to the ministry with limited conversation about your line of work.

5. **Let Men Be Men**

- A resourceful wife works closely with her husband, the Senior Pastor.
- The First Lady serves as his confidant and unofficial advisor in most cases.
- Do not use this influence to lord over your husband or the other men in the ministry. This is not good because it will run good people off.

6. **Accept Criticism & Conflict**

- Do not harbor resentment or hurt feelings when the criticism comes.
- No one is perfect.
- Pray about negative feedback and move forward in love.

7. **Relationships Matter**

- Accept the fact that some people are just difficult while maintaining a loving relationship with your church family.
- *"If it is possible, as much as depends on you, live peaceable with all men"* (Romans 12:18 NKJV).Love intentionally!

8. Learn from The Past

- Refrain from making the same mistakes repeatedly.
- Remember, one cannot keep doing the same thing desiring a different result.
- Be quick to forgive yourself & self-correct.

9. Live in the Present

- Do not waste time thinking about past mistakes.
- Extend grace to yourself as you oftentimes extend it to others.
- We all have bad days.

10. Trust God for the Future

- Remember, *"It is better to trust in the Lord than to put confidence in man."* (Psalm 118:8 NKJV)

- People mean well when they promise to support you until the end.
- Remember this truth, the masses left Jesus.

About the Author

Pastor Valerie Tripp Frazier lives in Raleigh, N.C. She has been actively involved in ministry for over 30 years in some capacity as either a teacher, volunteer, and Pastor. She has also served as the Women's & Associate Pastor of Kingdom Family International Church in Wake Forest, N.C. for the past 12 years. She has been the keynote speaker at International Conferences in Zimbabwe & Kenya, Africa with future plans to host additional conferences in Ghana & Zambia. She teaches a monthly Bible study for women, speaks at women conferences, and retreats across the globe.

Alongside Pastor Valerie Frazier's ministry associations, she has a Bachelor of Science in Business Management from North Carolina State University. She currently holds an Associate & Advanced Degree in Christian Ministry from Raleigh Institute of Biblical Studies.

Valerie Frazier is married to Pastor Rodney E. Frazier, Senior Pastor of Kingdom Family International Church, Wake Forest, N.C. They have two adult children Rodney E. Frazier, II and Christina Frazier Mason (Cadarreus). Pastor Valerie T. Frazier has a passion for rightfully dividing the word of God with truth so that the women of God can walk in the liberty that God promised.

Pastor Valerie Frazier, CCLC
Women's Pastor, Kingdom Family International Church
Certified Christian Life Coach
TEL: (919) 569-0357
FAX: (919) 400-9321
For more information on Pastor Valerie T. Frazier and her upcoming events visit:
www.valeriefrazier.org
www.kingdomfamily.church